POEMS;

BY

WALTER M. LINDSAY.

"A planet's shot, a shade which followeth,
A voice which vanisheth so soon as heard."

NEW YORK:
D. APPLETON & COMPANY,
346 & 348 BROADWAY.
1856.

CONTENTS.

PRELUDE.

Oh! memory, let thy pilgrim feet
Unto the shores of youth return!
Where golden sands and billows meet,
The morning lights have ceased to burn.

Walk silent in the evening gray,
And hear the voices of the sea
Repeat the story of a day,
That never shall return to thee!

BROOKDALE, N. Y., January, 1856.

THY PICTURE.

THE grace of childhood clings to thee,
  In thy maturing youth;
Thy woman looks are eloquent
  With purity and truth;
And, in thy gentle mien, there is
  The steadfastness of Ruth.

There have been locks of richer brown,
  And eyes as calmly bright,
And cheeks that blushed a rosier hue,
  And brows as marble white;
But never one, whose beauty stirred
  The heart to more delight.

Expression such as thine it was,—
As beautiful and mild,—
That, in the watches of the night,
Upon the painter smiled,
Beside his canvas dreaming of
Madonna and her Child.

Thy mind is like a placid stream,
Outspread beneath the sky,
That mirrors in its waters all
The changing world on high,—
The sun, the stars, the wandering cloud,
That slowly saileth by.

We are not wholly left of Heaven,
While such remain on earth,
Who from no human standard take
The measure of their worth,
But were created perfect by
The Hand that gave them birth.

THY NATURE AND MINE.

THOU enterest in the House of God,
  As freely as a child
Its father's presence ; for on thee
  The Holy One has smiled,
And, in thy breast, a dwelling made
  For nature undefiled.

Between thee and the hosts of heaven
  Is spread no sombre cloud ;
The angels answer to thy need,
  When thou in prayer art bowed.
Thy whisper, at the Holy gates
  Their lips repeat aloud.

But I—whene'er I seek to pray—
  Feel that the words alone
Have passed my lips. My heart within
  Is closed, as with a stone ;
And my sepulchred soul is left
  To make unheard its moan.

Unless an angel break the seal,
  And roll that stone away,
I shall until the end, remain
  In darkness, though the day
Break clearer in our common sky.
  Oh ! wherefore then delay !

THE SHIPWRECK.

Ah ! blame me not, if I have been
A shipwrecked man.
Thou canst not tell how strong the tide
And current ran.

The same sweet scenes are round thee now,
As in the past :
Thy sheltered ear has never heard
The ocean blast.

The slenderest bark can safely float
In waters still,
But whirlwinds, on the stoutest ship,
Must work their will.

I could not breast the wintry storm,
And, evermore,
Must make my home among the weeds
Upon the shore !

THY SOUL AT PRAYER.

This Sabbath morn, thy soul has made
  Anew its peace with heaven ;
Thy chamber is the temple, where
  Thy offerings are given.
And yet thou prayest, not alone
  At morn and evening hours ;
Thy holy thoughts to God ascend
  Always.—As the flowers
Unconscious of their sweetness are,
  Yet breathe it on the air
In all their day, so thy pure life
  Is an unceasing prayer.

TO THY MEMORY.

YES! thou art fair!
I had not thought
Again to be by passion wrought
To such excess of love,
But that, in absence, I could bear
A mind above
Its influence, and control
The movements of my soul.

As unto one,
Who hung, in other years,
A harp between the trees,
Which, silent long,
Again renews its melodies,
And wild aerial song,
My life to me appears!
Time has restrung
The loosened chords, and now among
The rocks and valleys wild,
Which all my pathways in the world beset,
I linger yet,
Again a child;
For angel songs are in my ear,
When thou art near!

COME FORTH.

Come forth, beneath the heaven,
While yet the sunlight in the sky
Shineth on the brow of even.
No shadow clouds thy gazing eye.
Behold the beauty of the earth!
The waters lie
Encompassed by a glorious frame
Of earth and sky!

In all, thy spirit is content.
    The absent are
Forgotten in the firmament !
    The evening star,—
The murmur of the Summer wind,—
    The leafy trees around,—
Are in thy silent heart enshrined.
    A deeper peace has found
Sweet access to thee, and thy breast
  Is calm as Nature in her rest !

HUMAN WEAKNESS.

As men toil up the mountain side,
  The weary day,
And from the top behold the sky,
  Yet far away ;
So holiest men, from youth to age,
  Make pilgrimage !

We may depart the valleys deep,
  And high ascend ;
But yet around us is the earth,
  Until the end.
Ourselves, alas ! we cannot raise
  Above our days !

THE DEAD BLOSSOM.

THE blossom died in early May,
  Before I knew its sweeter prime;
No mellow fruit upon the bough
  Shall hang in Autumn's harvest time.
Alone the naked tree shall stand,
Fruitless in the teeming land.

But when the Winter, chill and drear,
  Whirls the leaves on every side,
All shall then as naked be
  As the tree whose blossom died.
For in the Winter, none can say
Which has blossomed in the May.

MY HOPE.

Shall I reveal to thee my hope?
  It is that I may be
Soon conscious of thy maiden love:
  Then shall the darkened sea
Break glorious on the coasts of earth,—
  The freighted argosy
Shall spread its sails unto the wind,
And leave the barren past behind.

Perhaps to me the future wears
  A hue more bright than may
Adorn it, when the sun shall look
  Upon the noon of day;
But, to my hope, a golden orb
  Seems shining on the way,
Undimmed by all the clouds which lie
Thick strown beneath the morning sky.

THE SABBATH BELL.

How like a knell
Sounds the far off Sabbath bell!
Not unto me
The summons speaks an accent glad.
Eternity
Hath meaning sad
Unto my faint, prophetic soul!
The ages shall their circuit roll
In endless gloom.
From the low portals of the tomb,
I see the dark procession go,
Dumb in its ecstasy of woe!

Oh! Sabbath bell!
My weary ears remember thee!
Upon the swell
Of that uncertain, clouded sea,
Which bounds the voyage of our life,
My shallop rose and fell
In frolic glee,
When first thy echo came to me!
I did not heed thy warning note,
But hoisted sail,
And watched my shallop outward float.
Oh! spirit, wail
The long, long voyage from the shore,—
The wreck upon the sand!
Oh! spirit, wail the chance that bore
Me desolate to land!

Oh! Sabbath bell,
To me thou soundest as a knell!

For, wandering on the silent shore,
I look upon the sea,
And know that sorrow, evermore,
Companion is to me.
In shipwreck, it alone remained.
It points me to the ebbing wave,
It points me to the sand,
Where it, with spectre hand,
Is digging at my shallow grave !

MY LIFE.

As one may see the laden ship,
Moored near the shore
By slender cables, safely ride
The waters o'er,
While whirlwinds toss the sea to foam,—
My life abides.
Thy love is my sure anchorage:
The changing tides
Of circumstance but stretch the chain;
The ship floats safely on the main.

But all the coasts of Time are set
With rock-bound shores ;
And, if the slender cable broke,
The laboring oars
Unto the sea were stretched in vain.
The leaping wave
That spendeth now its force in spray,
Would to a grave,
Beneath the angry billows, bear
The laden ship that rideth there !

OH! COME.

OH! come to me in dreams to-night!
Beside me sleeping stand;
And bending, touch my troubled brow
With gentle hand!

My waking heart is weary with
Its longing watch for thee;
Oh! therefore in a vision come,
And look on me!

So came the angels, in the past,
To those who inly prayed;
And for thy coming, holiest wish
My soul has made!

MY DREAM.

How sweet were toil, if thou wouldst be
   Companion to my lot!
Beneath the heaviest burden then
   My soul would murmur not.

Nay, all the labor of the day
   Were lightened by the thought,
That each swift moment, to thy side
   My steps at evening brought.

The times, unto our converse left,
  Were stars within the sky
Of an unclouded Summer night,
  Sweet love! if thou wert nigh.

My many cares at evening hours,
  When all my toil was done,
Would gently rest, as folded flowers
  Await the morning sun!

MY WEALTH.

I AM not poor, with love like thine;
Thou art the sunshine of my heart;
My empty cup is brimmed with wine,
When I remember what thou art.

In thy sweet face my future lies,
Thy words an endless music are;
And hope has kindled in thine eyes,
The light that guides me near and far.

What though I own nor house, nor land,
Nor sway the minds of kindred men,
While I a wealth of heart command,
Which spent, returns to me again!

DO YOU REMEMBER?

Do you remember
One who wandered at your side,
In the dusk of eventide,
Many months ago,
While the snow
Yet lingered in the valley green?

The ember
Smoulders on the hearth, unseen,
Throughout the weary day,
When those, for whom it kindled first,
Are far away.
Thus I remember!

For thee,
The skies are calm and bright,
And to thy far-off sunset shall
Succeed a starry night.
But we shall be
Apart on life's unresting sea.

Like to an isle in Tropic seas,
For ever fair
Thy life shall stand ;
While we
The storm, or Summer breeze,
Alike shall bear
Yet farther from the land,
'Till some to-morrow's dawning light
Shall glance upon the troubled wave,
And here and there reveal a spar,
Tossed high above an ocean grave.

THY SORROWS.

THY sorrows are the ministers
  Of God unto thy soul.
They pour the drop of bitterness
  Into the golden bowl,
Whose sweetness, else, would steep thy
    heart,
  In worldly bliss alone.
Receive them as ambassadors,
  Sent from the Holy Throne
To the beloved of the earth,
  And, through the blinding tear,
The glory of their angel form
  Unto thee will appear.

THE WISH.

Forgive me, if, in sadder hours,
  I wish thy earthly path
Was not through sunshine and through
    flowers;
  For now thy journey hath
No need of a sustaining hand,—
  No need of friendly cheer;
A sunlit pathway, through the land,
  Leads on from year to year.

Hadst thou been born to other fate,
  And, wandering on alone,
Reached, with sad heart, the iron gate,
  Between whose portals shone
The watch-fires in the fields of life,
  How gladly had I then
Thy footsteps guided through the strife
  Of myriad struggling men!

HOW BEAUTIFUL THOU ART!

How beautiful thou art!
In the sad silence of an hour,
Wherein I knew my heart
Would never more on earth have power
To win confession of thy love,
Into my soul
Thy image sank; and though above
Its surface roll
The angry tides of human life,
Yet nature, in the endless strife,
Shall leave, untouched, the tender grace
Of thy remembered face.

How wild was that vain dream,
In which I thought thou wert mine own!
A moment, on the stream,
The shadow of my life was thrown,
And then it passed in sunlight on!
The buoyant tide
Remembered not the bared tree,
That drooped beside
Its waters, wandering to the sea,
But swept, in fuller beauty, free,
By castle wall, and fertile plain,
Unto the boundless main.

CONSIDER.

For some wise purpose, known in heaven,
  Thy life approached to mine;—
The full-orbed moon unto the sea.
  Upon the waters shine
Its rays, and swell them to a tide
  That will not more decline.

We cannot say unto the wave,—
  Break on the land no more,—
Although it crumble, day by day,
  Our dwelling on the shore,
And sweep, at last, in angry foam,
  The shattered roof-tree o'er.

ERROR IN LIFE.

I DO deceive myself, like unto him
  Who sees the clouds at even,
Crowned with the glory of the sun,
  Uprising in the heaven,
As battlements,—and dreams that far
  Within their shadow lies
The Holy City of our rest.
  Alas! how soon the skies

Are darkened by the hand of night!
  And he, who waited long
To see the golden gates unclose
  Before the heavenly throng,
Which should, once more, sing songs of
    peace,
  Shall, haply, only hear
The anthem of the gathering storm,
  In thunders chanted near,
And see the driving clouds enwrap
  The glory of the skies.
Such is the aspect of the heaven
  We watch with mortal eyes!

HOPE.

None are so lost on earth, but that
A final prayer
May win them mercy in the skies.
The judgment there
Is tempered with sublimest love.
Wherever cast,
And though a shipwreck thou hast made
Of all the past,
Yet may thy humbled soul uplift
A prayer to God,
Who pities ever those who bow
And kiss the rod.

DREAM ON.

DREAM on. I know thy visions fair
Find not their type in me.
The common form of life I bear.
No deeper mystery
Than lingers round the lives of all,
Attends my simple lot.
Mine is a nature to be known,—
And then,—to be forgot.

Thy heart would give its reverence to
  Some character, which rose
Above the earth. An Alpine peak,
  Crowned with eternal snows,
And glittering silent in the sun,
  Contents thy spirit more,
Than do the empty fields which lie
  Way-trodden at thy door.

So let them rest. For thee my hand
  Plucked up the weed and thorn,
And scattered wide the fruitful seed.
  But though the growth had borne
The harvest of a holier life,
  The change unto thine eye
Had brought no gladness ; therefore, let
  The grain unripened die !

Better the desert, with its drift
  Of parched and barren sand,—

Better the sterile rocks,—than see
  Such growth ungathered stand.
I care not much, if blight and storm
  Shall come and wither all.
Thou hast not cared, when they have
    bloomed,
  And wilt not, when they fall !

THOU KNOWEST NOT.

THOU canst not tell how strong and deep
  Thy hold on me has grown,
The ivy has sent down its roots
  To the foundation-stone;
And it will live, when rock and wall
  Alike are overthrown.

NO MORE.

My heart no more can clothe its hope
With drapery of dreams,
I have awakened to the truth.
How cold and sunless seems
The pathway of departing youth!
Our manhood is such day
As men in Arctic seasons know,
Where twilight's broken ray
Revealeth the unchanging snow.

No blush of Summer bloom,
No glory of the Spring is there,
The rugged lines of life appear
The deeper in the gloom.
The currents of the younger soul
Are frozen hard and fast:
The breath of passion changes to
A cutting wintry blast.
God help the wanderer who must go
This Arctic path alone,
And die within the wilderness,
Forgotten, or unknown.

THE LAST OF THE VINTAGE.

I EARLY gathered all the fruit
  Within the vineyards of my heart,
And filled and drained my cup, as if
  The new-found wine would ne'er depart.
And so I lived from day to day,
  Until I saw the lessening store,
And learned to know the vintage time
  Would come to me on earth no more.

Since that sad wisdom was revealed
  I watch with more than miser's art,
Whatever now remains of all
  Once stored within my burdened heart.
I dream, perchance, that what is left
  Has ripened, on the restless sea,
To richer worth, than all I spent
  In young and thoughtless revelry.

THE STREAM OF LIFE.

THE bubbling, shallow, noisy brook,
Late born in yonder grassy nook,
Leaps out into the open day,
Like to a frolic child at play.
A pebble throws it from its track,
Or rolls the limpid waters back;
And the small pressure of the hand
Its utmost efforts can withstand.

Yet, even in that circling play,
The channel wears a deeper way.
The neighboring streamlets downward glide,
And mingle with the growing tide.

The dew-drops from the evening sky,
Fall on its bosom silently ;
The Summer rain, the Winter snow
Are mingling in its calmer flow.

Between the hills the deepened stream
Soon wanders silent as a dream ;
Its waveless, but unresting tide
Crumbles the nearing mountain side.
How few who see the river's force,
Recall the fountain at its source,
And the small obstacles, that gave
A path to its resistless wave !

GONE.

I LOVE no more. The April flower
  Has withered in the Summer sun ;
It bloomed throughout its filling hour—
  The harvest time has now begun.
The fields of life encumbered stand,
  Perchance, with nobler growth to-day ;
And duty guides the laboring hand,
  From ruddy morn to twilight gray.

But yet, although the harvest yields
  Unto my toil a rich return,
I stand among the flowerless fields,
  And for the growths of April yearn.
The violet springing by the brook,
  Wild wandering downward to the sea,
Was lovelier, in its sheltered nook,
  Than are the harvest fields to me !

SINK TO THY REST.

Sink to thy rest, oh! glorious sun,
 And draw the veil of night
Around thy couch within the west!
 Hail! to the starry light
That trembles in the upper sky;
 And to the full-orbed moon,
That slow and silent wanders on
 Unto her silvered noon!

How like a Queen she reigns in heaven!
  Supreme in all the throng,
Whose choral voices yet repeat
  Creation's earliest song.
Look upward, through the boundless night,
  Oh! wondering soul of man,
And, to the breadth of endless space
  Compare life's narrow span!

A CALM UNKNOWN.

A calm, unknown for weary days,
  Upon my spirit fell,
While lingering by thee yesternight.
  It was as if the swell
 Of ocean broke no more
 In surges on the shore,
But silent touched the nearing land.
 I trust the Summer peace,
Then brooding o'er the waves of Time,
 May only know increase.

GRAVES.

I SOMETIMES stand at eventide,
Among a thousand dead,
Who were, by hands of those they loved,
Well sepulchred.

Many, I knew in other years,
When they and I were young;
With some have stood at close of day
These scenes among.

The marble tablet tells their worth,—
The sorrow of their friends.
With such brief record, all their tale
Of being ends.

I touch, with lingering hand, the grass
That o'er them richly grows ;
And mark their stature by the mounds
Which them enclose.

There are no footprints round about,
The dead are left alone.
The goal of man's affection, is
The burial stone.

Why wish for stately monuments
Above us, when we die !
The sad memorial only meets
The stranger's eye.

He reads the name with careless glance,
And then straightway departs.
The hands of men remember us,
But not their hearts.

As well the pauper's nameless grave,—
The sleep of friendless men,—
As be entombed in marble, and
Forgotten then!

THY FANCY IS.

THY fancy is, that he alone
  Can rule thy woman mind,
Whose nature hath to iron grown.
  Unto a will defined,
And absolute, thy love it seems
  Will wholly be resigned.

I cannot such a conqueror be ;
  I do not ask for power
O'er those I love.—As well assert
  Dominion o'er the flower
That fills with sweetness all the breath
  Of morning's purest hour.

It is no portion of the love
  Which in my heart I bear,
To master thy unbroken will,—
  It may its freedom wear.
The wider realm that love unfolds,
  With thee my life would share.

Nature has made thee equal to
  The proudest of us all,
In that high gift of intellect
  Which we our province call ;
And, though I bow'd in life to none,
  I could not thee enthrall.

My vision hath been to create
  Such sympathy of heart,
As will enable thee to bear
  On earth an equal part
Of joy and care alike.—For this
  Thou nobly fitted art.

I yield my being up to thee,
  As earth in silence lies
Beneath the arching heaven:
  Enriching from the skies,
In sunshine and in cloud alike,
  Its noblest treasuries.

WHEN I CONSIDER.

SOMETIMES, when I consider all
   The tumult and the stir
Of daily life;—how often Truth
   Mocks at the worshipper
Who cleaves unto her earthly robe;—
   How envy, pride and hate
Can poison deep the friendly cup,
   And closest hearts unmate;—
The sunshine seems to lose its light,
   And all the beauty fades
From hill and valley, from the fields,
   The sea, and forest shades.

WHY NOT CONTENT.

Oh! why is not thy soul content
    To let the future find
Its anchorage where now thou art!
    Else may the changing wind
  Part us upon the deep,
  Although my heart shall keep
Such watch as shipwrecked men maintain
    Upon a sail at sea;
For, unto vision lost, the hope
  Some storm-girt night may be!

THE JOURNEY OF LIFE.

How can a wanderer, far astray,
Discover where he missed his way,
When phantoms mock his straining sight,
And all the sky is dark with night !

At early morn, with buoyant heart,
They watched him from his home depart.
The April sky was calm and bright ;
The clouds were touched with rosy light :
And, in the shadow of the dawn,
The fading moonbeams glimmered wan.

He said it was a cloudless day ;
He could not miss his easy way :
That, long before the noon, his eye
The golden city would descry,
And he beneath its turrets dwell
Before the evening shadows fell.

A moment,—and the boy was gone
Across the rising ground ;
And then his footsteps mingled with
The multitude around.

The tears upon his earnest face
Too soon, alas! were dry,
So full of wonders was the place
That met his eager eye.
The busy crowd swept to and fro,
And sported on the track ;
Some onward ever seemed to go,
And some were loitering back.

'The way is rough and hard,' they said,
'We cannot climb the mountain's head;
And know not if the rugged height
Does not to other steeps invite.'

Again there came a goodly band
Of youths and maidens, hand in hand:
They stopped upon the neighboring green,
And danced the stalwart oaks between.

'The day is long; this calm retreat
Is sheltered from the noonday heat;
And, when the sun is sinking low,
Upon our journey we will go.
For why is all around so fair,
If none were meant to linger there?'

At morn he listened to the young,
And laughed and danced the gay among;
And when the sun was overhead,
He thought of what the elders said.

The mountain hourly seemed to grow
More distant to his weary gaze,
And, as he mused, the single path
Was hidden in the evening haze.

Far up, a lofty pinnacle
Gleamed in the fast departing light ;
A beacon, and a sigh of fear
Unto his unbelieving sight :
For there the temple glimmered through
The darkness of the growing night.

A beacon,—yet the day was past,
And all the valley deep,
Was shadowed in the silence of
A never-ending sleep.

The mother, standing at her door,
Saw not her erring offspring more :
Nor did the temple's opening gate
Receive the wanderer, coming late.

I HAVE BEEN HAPPY.

I HAVE been happy. Time has been,
When privilege of life
Was glorious to my bounding pulse ;
When all the eager strife
Of manly effort for the laurel crown,
Created in my soul
The joy of an Olympian game.
The chariots by me roll
While I stand idle on the earth,
For, unto me, the race
Has lost its charm :—I care not who
Attains the foremost place.

What matter if the strife were done!
What matter if the race were won!

Once I could live for self alone;—
        Once the applauding breath
Of multitudes, had even strown
        The path to early death
With flowers.—Once, beauty and the love
        Of woman, seemed to be
The ornaments of life, from which
        'Twere wiser to be free,
Save in the mirth of festal days.—
        Once Hope a vesture wore,
With jewels rich and Tyrian dyes.
        Such dreams return no more.
Were all mine own, my heart would bear
Only a larger weight of care!

THE DEATH OF THE YEAR.

The sober days of Autumn now
  Are garlanding the Year
With withered leaves and faded flowers,
  And grasses dead and sere.

The coronal of Spring is gone.
  The Summer's later glow
Has paled before the chilling wind,
  And in the early snow.

The Year is dying, day by day,
  And soon, a wintry night
Shall seal its closing vision to
  The darkness and the light.

It will not sleep in earthly grave,
  But every heart will bear
A portion of its ashes, in
  Our pilgrimage of care.

I LOVE THEE.

I LOVE thee, as the hunted hind
  Thirsts for the water brook,
When far across the desert sands
  She turns a weary look.
Sometimes, unto her straining eye,
  There seemeth to appear
A distant lake and palm-girt shore,
  But as she draweth near
The waters vanish in the sky,—
  The palms no more are seen.
She knows it was a vision, yet
  Her failing strength has been
Outworn upon the desert bare.
What wonder, if she dieth there!

TO THE PUREST.

THOU art within thy chamber dim.
  The slowly waning light
On darkness verges in the east.
  Beside the embers bright
Thou sittest long,—forgetful half
  If it be day or night.

Before thee is the open book
  Of God's revealèd word;
Upon it rest thy claspèd hands.
  No utterance has stirred
The silent breathing of thy lips,
  And yet thy prayer is heard.

Thou prayest that thy life may be
So ordered, that its end
Will find thy soul at peace with Heaven.
No earthly wishes blend
With holier thoughts. Untainted, all
Thy prayers to God ascend.

As Mary turned from all the world,
And suffered not its care
To come between her path and heaven,—
And could her beauty wear
Unconscious as the opening flower ;—
So thou, than whom more fair

Are none in all this glorious earth,
Canst see each troubled soul
Around thee, strew its path with thorns ;—
And, with a sweet control
Of all thyself, await in peace
Until the golden bowl

Is broken at the fount of life,—
  Until the silver cord
Is loosed between thee and the world.
  Thou knowest that thy Lord,
To whom such innocence is given,
  Will make thee thy reward.

I HAVE OUTWATCHED.

I HAVE outwatched the fires of life ;
They die upon the plain ;
And, in the darkness of the night,
The stars are seen again.

Mine were the beacon lights of earth ;
To ashes they have turned :
Yet, all the while, unwatched above,
The holy stars have burned !

Had I looked to their changeless light,
I had not gone astray,
Nor, in the dreary midnight, stood
Beside the ashes gray !

THY RULE.

THY spirit rules within my breast,
  A Queen upon the throne,
And all my silent thoughts obey
  Thy sovereignty alone.
Beloved, wherefore wilt thou not
  Receive me as thine own!

It may not be a regal sway,
  But never potentate
To nobler uses could command
  The government of state,
Or wield with more authority
  A willing subject's fate.

Oh! can it not suffice thy mind
  To have such sceptred sway?
Or art thou not content, unless
  The multitude obey,
And to thee, on a gilded throne,
  A ceaseless homage pay?

I think it not. Thy angel mind
  No worldly raiment wears,
Nor seeks, in pomp and circumstance,
  Increase of daily cares.
Embroidered only on thy breast,
  A Christian cross it bears.

Thou wilt not leave the throne whereon
  So long thy place has been;
But with a kinder rule wilt sway
  My heart, oh! Virgin Queen!
How desolate, if thou wert gone,
  Alas! were all within!

MY SOUL.

My soul for starless darkness longs.
  The night leaves memory free,
To people every empty heart
  With shapes that may not be
Discerned in light of common day.
  The grace of vanished youth,—
The loveliness of other days,
  Are then once more a truth.

A truth unto remembrance, though
  Upon life's desert way,
The flowers that longest bloomed have known
  At last a sure decay.

A truth, though none remain, whose love
  Gave beauty to the morn,
And though we stand at eve alone,
  Forsaken and forlorn.

Come, night, and draw thy dusky veil
  Across the arching sky;
I weary of the golden lights,
  Which on the meadows lie.
The glory of the earth to me
  Unreal splendor seems,
Akin to that magnificence
  Which cheats us in our dreams.

UNTO THE BROKEN HEART.

THERE is no beauty in the earth
Unto the broken heart.
The song of mirth
Is sadder than the dirge ;
And art
And its creations, seem
An empty dream.

The glory of the morning sky,—
The sun-lit trees,—
The shaded dells, and meadows near
To Summer seas,—

The chant of woodland songs,—
The waterfall,—
Are wrongs
Unto the eye and ear,
For they recall
The lost and dead
Who from our earthly paths have fled.

THIS APRIL MOON.

THIS April moon will tempt thee forth
  To stand beneath the sky :
No gloomy shadows of the night
  Upon the meadows lie.
A veil of beauty robes the earth.
  The distant waters are
Unto her breast a silver shield.
  Encrownèd by the star
She sleeps, and God above
Keeps watch with his eternal love.

Thine eyes are on the earth and heaven.
  Thy silent thoughts outpour
In solitude the breath of prayer.
  If life can e'er restore
The grace, which unto nature clave,
  When angels sang on high
The beauty of the new-born world,
  Thy spirit draweth nigh
Unto the type, created when
God walked among our fellow-men.

I cannot hope that in the calm
  Of thy deep thoughts, there came
Remembrance of my love, or yet
  A murmur of my name.
But if the wandering spirit may
  Its nearing presence tell,
My soul has whispered to thy ear.
  I trust the words may swell

The current of thy heart above
Its shores, and deepen it to love.

May angels guard thy rest to-night!
  Thy childlike sleep shall seal
Thy vision to the things of earth;
  But slumber shall reveal
The land, in which thy spirit dwells.
  I may not enter there:
And yet I trust thy lips, in dreams,
  Will breathe an earnest prayer,
That in this world, and that to come,
We both may find a common home.

I WATCH ALONE.

I WATCH alone this silent night,—
Alone, and yet
A thousand shapes are gliding near.
The dead have met
The living in the shadowy throng.
Forgotten years
Upon my head their ashes lay;
Forgotten tears
Their long-dried channels fill,
And flow at will.

I feel that I this phantom host
Could drive away,
And summon to my presence all
The bright array

Which Hope can marshal in her train.
But well I know
That all, around me gathered now,
Wore long ago
The beauty of the earth.
Behold its worth!

A little while, and I may be
Mourned with the rest:
The valley clods may crumble on
My pulseless breast.
A shadow of a bygone time,
My name may be;
And thou, perchance, in solitude
Mine image see;—
Recalling then the years,
I trust with tears.

WE ARE NOT MASTERS.

WE are not masters of the years ;
        Each Summer hour,
The current of our lives shrinks up,
        And loses power.
The full fresh tides of youthful thought,
        That channelled deep
Their course in earlier, happier days,
        Shall silent sleep
In mantling pools. The withered tree
        Will to the sun
Of Summer show its barèd boughs ;
        And, standing on

The meadows wide, the eye shall see
    The harvest field
So swept by time, that it may not
    To gleaners yield
Aught for the charities of life.
    The fields were sown
By hands forgotten.—The harvest was
    For Death alone.

OH ! PROPHET HEART.

OH ! prophet heart ! from early days
My sorrow was foretold
By thy deep utterance. The tide
Of human woe has rolled
Ceaseless upon the shores of life.
Sometimes a golden sun
Has lit the waters with its beams ;
But yet they broke upon
The shattered years, and spared them not.
In sunshine and in cloud,
Each fair young Hope that ventured forth,
Has gone unto a shroud.

Is there no sign of calmer seas !
  Thou watchman standing far
Above the mists of earth,—whose brow
  Is crownèd with the star
That shone on Bethlehem long ago,—
  Speak to the waters wild !
Remember all thy sorrows, Lord,
  When thou wert here a child.
Oh ! prophet heart ! thy mantle dark
  Upon his altars lay !
God stills the waters in their wrath,
  Whene'er his children pray !

DREAMING.

TO-NIGHT, while I sit dreaming here,
  Perchance thou art at prayer;
I would the roaming wind to me
  The murmured words would bear,
That I might know that thou hadst asked
  For me thy Father's care.

The world had laid upon my heart,
  For years, an iron hand,
And closed the gate from whence it looked
  Unto the spirit-land,
Until I thought I heard thy soul
  Beside the portal stand.

In that calm hour it opened to
  A glimpse of earth and sky,
Which shone as if an Eden came
  Unto the dreaming eye;
And my rapt soul in glory walked
  A brighter world on high.

I sudden woke from that sweet trance,
  And round me looked to find
The angel hand, whose touch had oped
  Such vision to the blind,
And brought a sunshine not of earth
  Unto my darkened mind.

It was a dream. The dark around
  To me no comfort brought;
The echo of a passing voice
  Lived only in my thought;
For some sweet strain that floated by,
  My prisoned soul had caught.

To-night, while I sit dreaming here;
  I know thou art at prayer ;
But, in the voiceless wish thy soul
  Breathes on the evening air,
The heart that loves thee best on earth,
  Alas ! has little share.

THE HISTORY.

As night by night, in other years,
  I lingered by thy side,
Methinks I might have known my heart
  Welled out a fuller tide,
And seen a freighted hope upon
  Its tranquil bosom glide.

The waters did not from the rock,
  As in a moment, flow.
It was no desert miracle.
  They gathered, dropping slow
From the long sealèd font, as if
  They were the melting snow.

Thine eye discerned the larger stream.
  Although thy heart was free,
And neither spoke, yet oft thy thought
  In silence turned to me.—
The rivulet to the river grew,
  Slow wandering to the sea.

Upon its waves, my mortal hopes
  Float onward to the deep.
No friendly hands the courses steer.—
  Thy thoughts in silence sleep,
While sorrow spreads the canvas torn,
  And cares the watches keep.

THE VOICE OF PRAYER.

The voice of prayer has ceased with me.
    The Holy gates above
Are closed unto the heart of him,
    Who made a human love
His arbiter for all the years.
    Unto that love was given,
Without return, the worship due
    To God alone in heaven.

And yet a love so deep and pure
    Deserved a better end.
I do not at my fate repine,
    For sorrow cannot mend

The broken links between our lives.
    My refuge is in pride ;
For gentler thoughts were trodden down,
    And in thy pathway died.

When men hereafter name my name,
    As one to feeling dead,
Remember who the final shaft
    Upon its errand sped.
If manhood be an early grave
    Unto my trusting soul,
At thy deep fountain broken was,
    For me, the golden bowl.

OH! MORNING STAR.

Why art thou hidden from my view,
    Oh! morning star,
That on Chaldean sages rose!
    Thy glories are
Unseen in all the heavens above!
    A Prince is born
Unto the nations of the earth;
    The creed outworn
Of worldliness is past and dead:
    I bear, within
My full-stored heart, the offering
    Of what has been

Most precious to my elder life,—
    The balm of love,
Grown pure in life's unwithered tree,—
    Yet look above,
And see no light revealed in heaven!
    Oh! morning star,
By watchful sages earliest seen,
    Shining afar,
Why falleth not thy light on me!
    I stand among
The fields of earth, nor hear the sounds
    Of angel song,
Ascending to the breaking dawn.
    The morn of grace is gone!

THE COMING SHADOW.

THE shadow of a day
That soon must come, upon me lies.
'Tis but a brief delay
Ere thou shalt stand with drooping eyes,
And, at God's altar, say
The words which give thy life away.

Within thy heart shall be
The gladness of a spirit blest;
No bitter memory
Shall wander nigh thy peaceful breast,

And happy in thy fate,
Unto the future all thy thoughts shall turn.
Before the golden gate,
Then opening wide, shall brightly burn
The myriad lamps of trust and love,
Lit by a glory from above.

I could not cloud thy joy,
Nor would I, if the power were mine.
My love hath no alloy
Of baser thought. I silent stand,
And see thee wander far
Beyond the grasp of my weak hand.
Thy beauty, as a star,
Shall rise upon another's even,
While I wait in the night,
And see no glory in the heaven.
I mourn the vanished sight
Of that fair Hope, which led me on,
And know it is for ever gone.

REMEMBRANCES.

My inward lookings only bring
  Her presence back to view,
Whom, when my life was in its Spring,
  In every pulse I knew.
How fair she looked, the greenwood shade,
  The Summer leaves among,
When, by the breath of evening swayed,
  Her loosened tresses hung!

I did not dream that she would look
  To other life than mine,
Though she was as the tranquil brook,
  And I the stormy brine.
Now wandering in the hills afar,
  Her path is hid from me,
Though earth and sky and polar star
  Therein may mirrored be.

THE HARVEST OF LIFE.

THE buds and blossoms of the Spring
  More beautiful appear,
Than all the harvest gathered in
  The Summer of the year.
But they who pluck the fragrant flower,
  And slight the ripened grain,
Shall mourn among the empty fields,
  In Autumn's sober wane.

The withered leaves, the broken stalk,
  The blossoms, dead and dry,
Recall no likeness to themselves
  Beneath the Summer sky.
And he, who made his harvest such,
  Can only mourn in vain ;
For never more in life we reap,
  When Autumn's on the wane.

MY SOUL IS DARK.

My soul is dark: I cannot see
  The path my feet should tread,
But hopeless walk the open road,
  The broader way instead,
Although I knew the sunless land
  To which it ever led.

Around me rise the mists of earth.
  I grope as in a cloud.
No answer comes unto my heart,
  Whene'er I cry aloud,
And every shape about me wears
  The likeness of a shroud.

I silent kneel to God in prayer,
  Alone, at dead of night,
And inly ask that there should shine
  For me the pillared light,
Whose radiance glimmered in the van
  Of Israel's dreary flight.

But all the dark unbroken is
  Unto my straining eye;
No light appears to break the gloom
  Of the o'erarching sky.
A rayless shadow only seems
  To me approaching nigh.

And yet I know an angel hand
  Is near me on my way,
Whose lightest touch my listening heart
  Would hasten to obey;
And it could lead me through the cloud
  Unto the open day.

An angel sent, I thought of Heaven,
To be my spirit guide,
To whom I have reached out my arms,
And called on every side ;
And yet, in all my sorrow, she
Has not to me replied.

Perchance she stands beneath the sky,
Herself in silent prayer,
Content with Nature, and its wealth
Of Earth, and light, and air,—
Forgetful of a parting soul,
While she is dreaming there.

So let her dream.—The time may come,
When she, awakened late,
Will feel that God appointed her
To influence my fate ;
Although, perchance, His providence
Would not the years await.

The years! who can foretell the end!
  In all the gloom I stand,
And hear the glass of time drop down
  The grains of golden sand,
And know not if I ever may
  Another year command!

Oh! God, why came this messenger
  To me in darkness near,
Unless she whisper words of hope
  Unto my listening ear;
And, with a holy counsel, seek
  My fainting heart to cheer!

RELIGION.

To me, Religion, thou art not
  In dark, ascetic habit clad.
  I hail thee as a spirit glad.
Thou hast transformed the lot
  Of martyrs, to a state
More glorious than a prince's realm.
    The darkest fate
That can our human life o'erwhelm,

Beneath thine eye
Will brighten, till the upper sky
Shows not a cloud.
The shroud,
When touched by thee is glorified,
And death defied.
The grave itself becomes a crystal gate,
Where we shall wait
In silent longing, till the bar
Is lifted high ;
And then, crowned by the Eastern star,
Enter the sky.

TO MY SOUL.

Why art thou vexed, my soul,
  With ceaseless lust of fame?
Nor honor, nor the pride
  Of an undying name,
Nor wealth, nor loud acclaim,
  Should be thy aim.

Look on the churchyard, and
  Among the nameless dead,
Behold the monument
  Above the great man's head.
His epitaph unread,
  And praise unsaid.

Better the simple mound,
  With grasses wild o'ergrown,
Than sculptured bust, or urn
  Of monumental stone,
If, to thy God alone,
  Thy worth was known.

THE DEAD.

THE ploughshare may thy hillock turn,
  The corn about it grow,
The rustic bind the golden sheaf
  Above thee lying low.

The sun may glimmer on thy bones,
  And they neglected lie,
And bleach in every Wintry wind,
  And every Summer sky.

It is as well for thee that such
  Should be thy body's doom,
As if it lay in sculptured vault,
  In deep cathedral gloom.

SOLITARY PRAYER.

HERE, in this solemn depth of wood,
Away from human eyes,
My heart an altar makes.
No worldly thoughts intrude.
Above me are the skies.
The breath of Summer wakes
Among the leaves a mournful air,
Like to the cadence of a prayer.

I know an early promise came,
That God would be
Where two or three
Were gathered in His name.
But, as the Saviour went apart
To solitary prayer,
And poured his troubled spirit out
Unto the midnight air,
When not a human eye could see
His agony,—
So would I, in this lonely place,
Come nearer to my Father's face.

PRAYER.

Bend beneath thy sorrow deep,
  Bend,—but do not break;
Unto Hope's reviving light
  Thy burdened heart shall wake.

God does not on our spirits lay
  More than we should bear,
But looks to see us ask His help
  In unceasing prayer.

Thou shalt not need to wait on Him
  As courtiers wait on kings,
Until an answer, long deferred,
  A slender solace brings.

Thy lonely chamber is a court,
  Whence thou canst see His face.
The sovereign Lord of all the world
  Is near in every place.

THE PLOUGHSHARE.

THE ploughshare driveth o'er the field,—
The single flower
That upward springs to greet the sun,
Beholds the hour
Of its untimely death at hand.
What though the grain,
In some far distant Summer, yield
Return upon
The broader stretch of broken land!
I shall repine
That the fair flower no more is mine!

A WINTER NIGHT.

The Earth is dead. Beneath the snow
It lieth in a winding sheet;
And all who look upon its face,
Go and return with muffled feet.

The sad night-wind its requiem sings;
The Winter robes it for the tomb;
And silent stars burn funeral lights
Above it, in the deepening gloom.

I KNOW AT LAST.

I know at last that thou art not
  Appointed for my guide ;
Thy gentle heart will never more
  To mine seem close allied.
I look upon thy love, and feel
  It is a falling tide.

It was a dream too full of joy,
  To last until the day
Its glory in the darkness came,—
  In darkness passed away,
And left me, sleepless, to await
  The morning cold and gray.

I would the common day were near,
  And that the strife and din
Of struggling men were heard alone
  My weary heart within,
That I might mingle with the crowd,
  Forgetting what has been.

Why seemed the arching heaven above
  To open unto me,
And holy angels to descend,
  If in the dawn I see
No sign of promise, and around
  The desert only be !

The desert, and its glittering sand,
  Spread out beneath the sky,-
Unbroken by the golden palm,—
  No well of water nigh,—
Where, when the weary traveller halts,
  He only halts to die !

TO MY SOUL.

Wherefore art thou sad, my soul,
  And burdened by thy care?
This is thy appointed grief,—
  The burden thou must bear.

The narrow pathway to thy God
  Is margined by the thorn.
The heart is lifted up to Heaven,
  From a world forlorn.

Mourn not that His will has hushed
  The voices heard in youth.
Their well loved music filled thy ears,
  And closed thy heart to truth.

Now, in the dark and silent night,
  The angels round thee stand,
And long loved faces seem to look
  From out the spirit land.

Let not the green grass on the earth
  Thy hope with fear affright ;
It is the curtain which conceals
  An Eden from thy sight.

IT IS NOT LIFE.

It is not life to stand alone,
  Upon this wide-spread earth,
Beside an altar overthrown.—
  The privilege is worth
No more, than, to the broken stone,
  Remembrance that it bore
Once the holiest sacrifice;
  Though never, never more
Shall Priest, or Priestess, minister
  Before the empty shrine.
The sacred chalice shattered is,
  And wasted is the wine.

The desert sands untrodden lie.
  What, though in elder days,
There rose, to a serener sky,
  The choral song of praise!
The oracles of life are dumb.
  With saddest accent plead,
No voice shall from the temple come
  To answer to thy need.
It is not life to stand alone,
Beside thy altar's broken stone.

THE TIDE OF ANGER.

The tide of anger runs not long in me.
  Its force, constrained, is spent
Upon the barriers of a soul,
  In trials more content
To bear misfortune, than to chide.
  The utterance of grief,
Rising in wild reproach, to me
  Affordeth not relief.

I shall not break our slender bonds,
  Because they will not bear
The burden of a common life.
  We cannot always share
With whom we will our mortal fate.
  An unseen spirit sways
Our destiny in this: and he is wise,
  Who silently obeys.

Unto such sad decree my soul submits,—
  Submits with bitter tears,—
For I behold a lonely path,
  On which the spectre years
Stand, joyless, waiting till I pass;
  With crowns of withered flowers
In mockery set upon the glass,
  With which they count the hours.

I fear to loose my hand from thine.
  While yet it may remain,

An Eastern star seems shining on
  The rock-bound desert plain.
Oh! heavenly Father! wherefore was
  Withheld from me such guide,
With whom my soul was well content
  To walk the desert wide!

FAREWELL.

FAREWELL,—we stand upon the verge
Of that last hour
Which ends the journey of the past.
I have not power
To stay the purpose of thy heart.
Thy fixèd will
Unto my saddest utterance speaks,—
Peace and be still.

Peace lest the sweetness of thy calm
Should broken be.
Peace lest the whisper of the world
Approach to thee.
Thou wishest that my love should die,
And make no sign.
A silent unseen martyrdom,
Thou wouldst have mine.

Thou askest of me to forget,—
Forget, and be
A gay companion on the path
Of life to thee,
Cheering thy spirit with my mirth.
Oh! would that I
Could tutor thus my scattered hopes,
Or from thee fly.

Could fly, and carry not the links,
Left broken in

My wounded heart, and think no more
    Of what has been.
But cankering there shall they remain !
    Remain to tell
The story known unto my life,
    Alas ! too well.

Unconsciously hast thou filled up
    Unto the brim,
With bitterness, life's single cup ;
    The vision dim
Of gladness, with unsparing hand,
    Hast driven far :
And clouded, in the heaven of life,
    The single star.

THE SABBATH MORN.

THE Sabbath morn should be
The halting station on the road of life,
Where to our armor we
May look, and test it for the morrow's strife.

The battle of the world
Should not encroach upon this time of rest:
With all our standards furled,
We should remove the corslet from the breast.

And standing silent then,
Beneath the cope of the o'erhanging sky,
Remember that all men,—
The victors and the vanquished,—all must die.

The trophies, which we gain
In the wild struggle,—fighting hand to hand,—
Shall not our souls maintain,
When entering naked in the spirit land.

For soldiers of the cross
We are not; but unto that host belong,
Whose victory is loss,—
Enlisted ever on the side of wrong.

While, therefore, on the way
We halt to try upon the Sabbath morn
Our armor for the fray,
Let us consider why the helm is worn.

Better the olive leaf
Should, with the myrtle, deck thy humble brow,
Than be an armèd chief
Among the hosts that look upon thee now.

THE VOYAGE OF LIFE.

THE child, beside his mother's knee,
Knows little of the open sea.
In a secluded vale he dwells,
Where golden sands, and smooth-lipped shells
        Amuse his life ;
Unconscious that the whirlwinds sweep
The surface of the outer deep,
        With never-ending strife.

        He sees, perchance,
Some bark upon the shore,
        Which sailed of late
        The waters o'er.

The broken spars, the rifted deck,
The silence of the wave-washed wreck,
Impress his heart;
But, in the sunshine on the sea,
And Summer breezes blowing free,
Such thoughts depart.

The sturdy oak is growing near,
The ash within the forest stands,
And yet he builds an osier bark,
Secured with silken bands.
The pennants gay
Stream from the mast,
As on the outward tide he floats,
Receding fast.

Oh ! mother, who hast known
The terrors of the sea,
In all the watches of the night
How thinks thy son of thee,

Who, smiling stood upon the strand,
And sent him helpless from the land.

What wonder, when a time
  Of looking out is past,
Some sad memorial of his fate
  Upon the shore is cast!—
    And that he,
    Gone down at sea,
Is lost to earth and all its memory!

EARLY DEATH.

MOURN not sweet soul, that death appeared
Unto thee while the sky
Yet brightened to the perfect noon.
It seemeth hard to die,
When earth is opening wide the gate
Unto the golden light,
And Summer gladness of the young.
And yet such early flight
Is sweeter, than when we remain
To see the sunshine wane,
And darkness gather on the earth ;—

The night, wherein we are
  Unguided by a star!
Mourn not sweet soul that death appeared
  Unto thee, ere the day
Had lost its gladness,—while the flowers
  Knew not as yet decay.

A LITTLE WHILE.

A LITTLE while, and we may meet ;
  And that one hour
Be unto all the growing time,
  As the fair flower
Unto the green and leafy stem,—
  A crowning diadem.

A little while, and we may meet ;
  And that one hour
Be unto all the passèd time,
  As the dead flower
Unto the dry and leafless stem,—
  A broken diadem.

IF HOLY ANGELS.

If holy angels spread their wings
  Around on every side,
And minister to human life,
  Why wanders, far and wide
From heavenly paths my erring soul!
  It stands with listening ear,—
Lost in the labyrinth of the world,—
  For some sweet whisper near,

Which shall direct its way aright ;—
  But none, alas ! is heard.
I know such spirit wandered by,
  For all the silence stirred
To music, as I breathless stood.
  But to my earnest prayer
No answer came.—The echo died
  Upon the desert bare.

IT IS A YEAR.

Yes! it is a year,
Since, in my heart, first kindled were
The lights of Hope and Love.
The passing Time has tried thy soul.
Thou canst not move
The golden hinges from their rest.
I stand without thy closèd breast,—
The gates will never open roll.

Yes ! it is a year,
And brief to thee such season seems,
For thou art nursed in Summer dreams,
And days appear
As moments to thy sleeping soul.
To thee my love in visions came,—
From thee in visions went,—
And other dreams thy mind control.
As one in water writes a name,
While cloudless skies are bent
Above,—thy heart recorded mine.
'Twas writ upon a Summer's day,
And in the sunlight passed away.
Unruffled now the waters shine.

Yes, it is a year !
To me a time of weary thought.
The present from the future brought
No charm against the sorrow near.

In silent toil
My life has burned its waning oil,
And other lights are gone!
How slowly have the lingering days
Swept by in laggard flight!
How cheerlessly the evening rays
Are yielding to the night!
I wonder, looking on
The way I came, that human eyes
Could blinded thus remain.
But what is wisdom worth, when Time
Can come no more again!

Yes, it is a year!
A year, that hath its Spring-time known,—
Its sweet and flowering May,—
Its silent Summer,—and at last
Its Autumn day;
And, in the Winter now, its life
Has passed away.

THY LIFE.

EARTH has no fountain in her breast
  To match the hidden well,
From which the waters of thy life
  In stainless beauty swell,
Sweet flowing from thy inner heart,
  As from a crystal cell.

But yet its calm and silvery course
  Would vanish like a dream,
If through its quiet channel swept
  That dark and turbid stream,
Upon whose wreck-strewn surface, sleeps
  No golden Summer beam.

Thy gentler course shall softly glide
  The purple hills among,
As pure as when the waters first
  To light and motion sprung,
Revealing ever in their depth
  The sky above thee hung.

I AM NOT FREE.

I am not free from taint of wrong.
  Nay, mingling with the flow
Of purest thought, are elements,
  Which, to my vision, show
The grosser soil of human life.
  Thus will the current glide,
Until the waters reach the sea,
  Unless the fuller tide
Within some peaceful valley swim,
  And, slowlier moving, be
By its own strength and nature's calm
  Restored to purity.

Thy thoughts would be the stately hills
Beside its tranquil way ;
Thy love would, on its silent depths,
Shine like a starry ray ;
And by its verge the flowerets spring.
Oh ! wherefore should it be
For ever wandering through the sands,
To mingle with the sea !
Better the fountain at its source
In other years had dried,
Than that the desert thus should be
Swept by its fuller tide !

OH! TREE OF KNOWLEDGE!

SAD tree of knowledge! from thy bough,
In Summers gone,
The golden fruit in beauty hung.
I gazed upon
Its sweetness in the night and morn.
My soul was won
To touch it by the angel near.
Yet, though to me,
It opened holier views of life,
Mine eye must see
The radiant gates of Eden closed,
Eternally.

TO HOME RETURNED.

THOU art to us returned again.
    To me it seems
As if in all thy absence I
    Had walked in dreams ;
For day was shorn of golden light,
    And all the hours,
Slowly and sad, went wandering by.
    No crowning flowers
The hand of Spring upon them cast.
    Cowlèd were they
As mourners, who unto a grave
    Bore Time away.

Yet now that we can meet once more,—
        In happiness,—
True children of the Summer light,
        They onward press,
Singing sweet carols in their glee.
        From morn till eve
They fill my heart with silent joy,
        And chaplets weave
From such sweet growths as Hope will bring.
        Yet, who can say,
If these will cheer my heart in all
        The Summer day!

I HAVE NOT SEEN THEE.

I HAVE not seen thee, yet I know
That thou art near :
Thy presence as the sunshine comes
Upon the year,
That else, in hues of sadness would
To me appear.

I have watched for thee, as we look
In early Spring
To see the sweet bird on the bough
Its carol sing,
While field and greening tree around
Are blossoming.

To me, thou as the Spring-time art.
Thy thoughts are showers
That, falling on my barren heart,
Put forth in flowers,
Until a radiant grace has filled
The happy hours.

I have not seen thee, yet I feel
That thou art near,
And brightest Summer lends its charm
Unto the year.
To me, of Hope the coronal
Thou dost appear.

UNMOVED WE SEE.

UNMOVED, we see the floweret die,
  Before its open leaves
Have caught the glory of the sky.
  Unmoved, in Summer eves,
We watch the clouds in darkness hide
  The myriad stars, which burn
Their heavenly watch-fires far and wide.
  The floweret shall return
In beauty to another Spring;
  The clouds, on other nights,
Will shadow not with dusky wing
  God's glorious beacon lights.

But, not unmoved, we see decay
  The growth, the spirit bears
Before our manhood fades away.
  Among the tangled cares
Of life, the single flower is born.
  Alas! the barren earth
In its creation is outworn;
  And all the after worth
Of Time, is counted by a hand
  That toils in endless pain,
But cannot, to the barren land,
  Bring back its growth again.

Oh! not unmoved the heart remains
  When we in darkness are.
One single night, upon the plains
  Of earth, we watch the star,
Which is in seeming promise sent.
  If clouds obscure its ray

In that brief time, our watch is spent.
  For the eternal day
Which cometh after, will not wane
  Unto another night.
The star, beheld from earth, again
  Will never meet our sight.

THE HEART IS SELFISH.

THE heart is selfish in its love ;
  It brooks no presence near
The throne on which it fain would rule,
  And, with unquiet ear,
Harks to a stranger's whispered name.
  What wonder is it then,
If a deep sadness fills its realm,
  Whene'er we see again,
Returning to assert its sway,
Some impulse of an earlier day !

I know that I ungently deal
  With thee in all my life ;
And yet, God knows, my nature hath
  Maintained an earnest strife
Against the impulse of its love.
  And that I love thee, thou
Wilt know before the time has cast
  One shadow on thy brow.
One shadow ! will that shadow be
A tribute to my memory !

Alas ! for him, whose love lay hid,—
  As, in the Wintry snow,
The floweret sleepeth till the Spring !
  If some untimely glow
Melt the white cerements of its bloom,
  The slender stalk shall rise
And blossom in the sunshine, which
  A moment fills the skies.

Shall blossom, but its opening breath
Assures the floweret's early death.

Mine is no thought of covert blame,—
No murmur of despair.
A silent blessing greets thy name,—
Thy name is all my prayer.
To me, thou art the goal of life ;
To me, its only prize.
I shall not win thee. Can I stand
And see, with tearless eyes,
Another pass me in the race,
On whom is turned thy thoughtful face ?

There is no wisdom in this cry
Of pain, at midnight hours.
When once the sudden frost has touched
The earth's untimely flowers,
What sorrow will their bloom restore !
But why bewail the dead,

Who long have dwelt within our hearts,
  If we no tears shall shed
O'er vanished hopes, whose promise brought
God's Eden home unto our thought!

UPON THE THRESHOLD.

Upon the threshold of my life
  A glorious vision stands ;
It pauses ere it wanders forth,
  And vainly clasps its hands.
In sorrow clasps them, as it goes.
  It goes to come no more,
Unless its memory haunt my soul
  Upon death's silent shore.

A glorious vision, born to me
  When life was in its prime,
And yet reviving all the grace
  Which blessed an earlier time!
Within my rugged heart it grew,
  Perchance a guest unmeet,
Though flowerets, in that lonely place,
  Sprang up beneath its feet.

I know not why, but all is changed.
  A glorious vision stands
Upon the threshold of my life,
  And vainly clasps its hands.
In sorrow clasps them, as it goes;
  For it will come no more,
Although its memory haunt my soul
  Upon death's silent shore.

I STOOD ALONE.

I STOOD alone, within the night,
  And watched the taper's beam
In thy near chamber dimly burn.
  Alone, and yet a dream
Came wandering to me in the gloom.
  I saw a thoughtful face,
With eyes intent upon the air,
  Watch in that silent place,
As if old memories came and went,
  Beheld by it alone.

Sometimes the light of happy smiles
  Upon her brow was thrown,
As if the wayward phantoms breathed
  The songs of earlier years,—
The songs, Youth sings unto the soul,
  While yet we know not tears!

Then would the fleeting brightness fade.
  Such music passed away,
And, to her heart, a sadder voice,
  Sang of a later day,–
A day that cometh to us all,—
  When sorrow standeth by,
Uncrowning all the golden hours,
  As over us they fly!

A sweeter calm to her returned,
  And, in the deeper night,
I saw, in her uplifted eyes,
  The glory of a light,

That cometh not from sun, or star.
  Before the voice of prayer,
The thronging phantoms fled away,
  And left, upon the air,
No echo of their changing lay.
  Peace had again returned
Unto her soul; and, in its depths,
  God's altar only burned.

IN VAIN.

I RAISE unquiet eyes to heaven,
  But dark its glories are ;
In all the gloom of night shines forth
  No solitary star.
The faint and flickering lights of earth
  Gleam in the valley far.

Each moment, as my steps ascend,
  The path more barren grows ;
The distant laurels cheer me not,
  I miss the valley rose :
No floweret blooms upon the edge
  Of these unkindly snows.

Ah ! had I dwelt in lowlier thoughts,
  A happier life were mine !
Faith had relit her holy fire
  In the deserted shrine,
And bade me, to a calmer thought,
  My purposes resign.

THE CLOUD.

A CLOUD envelopes earth and sky.
  This dark and dreary day
Were emblem fit of life to me,
  But that to-morrow may
The glory to the sky restore,
  And to the earth its grace,
While my sad soul no light discerns
  Within its darkened place.

Fate has its sharpest arrows sent.
  The bulwark of my pride,
Cast down in an unequal strife,
  Is shattered far and wide,
And in the breach I silent stand.
  Yet were my courage high,
But that I see it matters not
  If I should fight, or fly.

Oh ! fatal hour, when first to me
  At morn thy beauty came !
Oh ! fatal hour, when first I dwelt
  In thought upon thy name !
Oh ! yet more fatal time than all,
  When, in a year gone by,
That love was born, which in thy ear
  Breathed out its earliest cry.

To thee, that night, my inmost soul
  Was opened as to God ;

With thee, that night, in happiness,
  The paths of earth I trod.
So near me came thy glorious love,
  That, in its fervent breath,
My heart leaped up to greet its life,
  And dreamed not of its death.

Yet even then a memory
  Was echoing in thy heart!
Thy steps drew near me only that
  They might from me depart!
They leave me on the fields of life
  Where I its toils began!
They leave me, if I know my doom,
  On earth a hopeless man!

The voice of sorrow has not strength
  To reach the happier ear:
Thy heart, in peace, the bitterest cry
  My lips can breathe, would hear.

While I in thy calm presence stood,
  Thou couldst foresee the day
Thy maiden hand, in other troth
  Would give thy love away.

What matter when these years shall end!
  Perchance it is a crime,
To see but sorrow in the space
  Of God's appointed time,
And fold our hands in dull despair.
  But if the end shall be
The severance of thy lot from mine,
  No joy is left for me.

The years have left but one desire.
  When it shall live in vain,
I care not if the lamp of life
  To sudden darkness wane.

If we shall part,—the bitterest chance
  That e'er my life beset,
Were blessing to the woe, which came
  Because our pathways met.

THE WATCHES OF THE NIGHT.

How many lonely eves have I
Watched in this silent place,
And, through the darkness, dimly seen
That well remembered face,
Whose lineaments are graven on
The tablets of my heart.
Oh! memory, to the happy thou
A sweet enchantress art,
Restoring to the years their bloom,—
Unto the past its grace,—
And bringing sunshine back again
Unto the darkened place.

But there are hearts, upon whose May
  Thick fell the whirling snow ;
And, in the early Autumn, such
  Forget the Summer's glow,
And sorrow for their withered Spring.
  They feel that manhood's prime
Was saddened by the blight, which came
  Upon an earlier time.

Alas ! it is too surely true
  That, by the hand of fate,
The key note of our lives is struck,
  While yet our souls await
The opening of the iron doors
  Upon the road of life.
The few to gentlest music move,
  The many hear the strife
Their souls must make with sorrow, in
  The low discordant cry,

Wrung from their trembling heart-strings,
while
To childhood they are nigh.
A pause there may be in such strain,
But woe to him, who hears
In that sad space, a gentler song.
He shall renew, in tears,
His toil among the empty fields
Of God's ungathered years.

In distant lands, where leafy palms
Rise in a barren clime,
The wanderer, musing at their feet,
Can hear the far-off chime
Of Sabbath bells, across the waste.
The sounds of earth and air
By memory are wrought, until,
To the sad heart, they bear
A likeness to the sounds of home :
And he can sink to rest,

Beyond the surges of the sea,
  With echoes thrilling by,
That seem to wander from a home
  Beneath his native sky.

But there are wanderers, where the palm
  Breaks not the drifting sand,—
Whose feet are loneliest, when they walk
  Within their native land :—
To whom the chime of Sabbath bells,
  Heard in the evening air,
Summons a shadow from the past,
  And not their souls to prayer.
Wanderers are these homeless men,
  Who sit beside their hearth,
As homeless, for their need of love,
  As any on the earth.

Oh ! memory, to the happy thou
  A sweet enchantress art,

But all thy sorcery is denied
  Unto the saddened heart.
Her face I see in all the hours,
  It cometh as the dream
Our Parents knew, when never more,
  By wood and sunlit stream,
In Eden they in gladness dwelt!
  Within the desert place,
The glory of that Eden fell
  Upon each sleeping face,
To mock the waking vision with
  A world that lay around,
When all the glorious sunlight shone
  Upon accursed ground.
Woe to the memory which restores
  An Eden to the heart,
When angels watch the closèd gates,
  And only say—Depart!

MY LOVE NO SOLACE IS.

My love no solace brings to thee,
  Thy heart is closed unto
The tribute poor. Before the gate,
  And in the common view,
To thee I have an offering made,
  But the unopened door
Received it not; and in the dust
  It lieth evermore.

It was no gift of royal price.
  No broidered altar cloth,—
No title to a fair domain,—
  Was earnest of my troth:

It was a simple manly love,
  Which, like an Alpine flower,
Among the snows, had blossomed in
  The sunshine of an hour.

Twas all I had.—I could no more.
  And while the fresher hue
Remained, I know the perfume stole
  The closèd lattice through,
And wooed thy wandering footsteps near.
  Near, while the morning breath
Its sweetness wasted on the air,—
  Aye,—wasted to its death.

Within the dust the offering lies !
  I watch, with folded hands,
The withered leaves, half lost to view
  Beneath the drifting sands.
I know that if the ópening flower
  Could thus neglected lie,

In all the time it shall remain,
  Till it, unnoticed, die.

Die,—while a fuller sunshine falls
  Upon thy maiden life!
Die,—ere my weary steps return
  Unto the endless strife
Which I with fate and fortune make!
  Die,—while other flowers
Are garlanded by happier hands,
  To grace thy bridal hours!

Then shall the closèd gates unbar,
  And thou with angel grace,
Companioned, on thy pathway go.
  Remembrance will not trace
My footprints in the sands of life.
  And, on such sunlit day,
The breath of thy full joy will bear
  All withered leaves away.

Yet all things, which have lived, remain !
  Remain, although the years
Oblivion promise, as they go,
  And though the past appears
Unto us a forgotten dream !
  Remembrance will not die !
And, in a day to come, our past
  Will cloud thy thoughtful eye.

Will cloud it, though I blame thee not !
  For, by the closèd gate
Of thy young life, I silent stand :
  Accepting, as my fate,
The withering of life's single flower,
  And, turning to depart,
With only blessings echoing in
  The silence of my heart.

MY VISION.

We were not friends in childhood.
  She to beauty grew
Far from the maze of wildwood,
  My footsteps struggled through.

Rent by the thorn,—
Slow climbing o'er the fallen tree,—
With heart outworn
By long expectancy

Of open fields and sunlit streams,—
  Upon such Eden space I came,
And saw the vision of my dreams,
  And breathed her name.

  In the golden eventide
We wandered through the meadows wide.

Would you behold that vision fair!
  Think not of starry eyes,
Nor marble brow, nor clustering hair,
  Nor blush of sunset skies
Mantling in the cheek of youth.
  Upon her thoughtful face,
Enthronèd sat the purer grace,
That cometh of angelic truth.

Oh! balmiest eves!
When in the lonely woodland, we
Beheld the leaves
Stir in their slumber silently,

As the low night-wind trembled by,
And wandered home,
With stars dim shining on our way.
Thrice have come
Autumnal shadows since that day.

Autumnal shadows! yet before
Each Autumn came a Spring,—
A Spring that shall return no more!
———Whose blossoming
Gave promise of a golden fruit.
I know not why,
But yet a canker to the root
Came ever nigh.
I saw, beneath each Summer sky,
The blossoms die!

Such is the worth,
That crowns the promise of the earth!

There is, upon the Summer air,
A breath of Winter flying past.
The forest walks, we trod, are bare.
Its leaves are scattered on the blast.
Our footsteps never more
Shall wander by the willowed shore
Of that shallow, rippling stream,
Whose music mingles with my dream

Time with trembling hands,
Counts the last grains of golden sands.
The tangled maze of wildwood,—
The wearied heart of childhood,—
The glimpse of fields and sunny streams,—
Are now as dreams.
The wintry time of life is near!
And never in another year,
To me that vision will appear!

Upon the open plain,
I see the sunlight wane,
Wane,—to come no more again!
The fields, the snow shroud only wear.

Life will never know
The melting of that shrouding snow!

WE MAY BE PARTED.

We may be parted. Changing winds,
Upon the tossing sea,
Leave each alone in all the day.
Yet shall the haven be
Unto our wandering barks the same.
Near to the calmer shore,
My lonely heart shall watch the deep,
And wait thee evermore.

Thou art upon the waves alone.
Alone,—and yet on high
God sets the signal of thy course
Within a cloudless sky;
The larger sun of Holy Truth,—
Which ever brighter grows,
As round about our mortal path,
The earthly shadows close.

We may be parted, yet I watch
Beside the calmer shore,
To see the lifting of thy sail
The far horizon o'er.
The changeless beacon lights of heaven,—
The breath of God,—will be
The polar star,—the steady wind,—
To bring thee unto me.

THE DEATH OF HOPE.

WITHIN the chambers of my heart,
  Hope, weak and fainting, lies.
My silent thoughts in sorrow look
  Upon her as she dies.
They wait, until she breathes no more,
  To close her glazing eyes.

There is no mark of age upon
  Her wan and pallid face.

Her beauty, though by sorrow dimmed,
  Retains the olden trace,
Which to her mien in childhood gave
  A more than angel grace.

She is not old, and yet the tears
  Have frequent channels worn
In that fair cheek, whose color once
  Flushed like the Early Morn,
When, in her chamber in the East,
  The infant day is born.

She is not old, and yet her thread
  Of mortal life is spun.
The sands within her broken glass,
  Once golden in the sun,
Drop slowly in the darkness, and
  At last have ceased to run.

Within the chambers of my heart,
  Hope now is lying dead.

My speechless thoughts in sorrow leave
  Their rising tears unshed,
And close the chambers evermore,
  Where she is sepulchred.

CONCLUSION.

Here, Memory, pause with folded hands,
And to the Past return no more.
Oh! why recall the golden sands,
The dream upon the Ocean shore.

The Summer time, in which was set
The sail unto the favoring breeze,
Hath to the Autumn changed, and yet
There is no sign of halcyon seas.

Here, Memory, pause with folded hands,
And to the Past return no more,
For never shall its golden sands
Renew the footprints on the shore.

www.ingramcontent.com/pod-product-compliance
Lightning Source LLC
LaVergne TN
LVHW011217110826
845150LV00006B/1453

* 9 7 8 1 4 2 5 5 1 6 7 3 4 *